MW00785718

Word to the Wise

Transformation Station

Production By:

NEKISHA COSEY MINISTRIES

Edited By: Nekisha Cosey

ISBN: 979-8-9877222-0-6

Book production: Nekisha Cosey Ministries.

<u>DEDICATION</u>

This book is dedicated to my Daddy, James Edward Massey Sr. (June 16, 1949-December 9, 2020. Thank you for loving me and being the greatest Father a girl could have. You are missed beyond measure.

My Mom, Minister Cornelius Goston. Thank you for making me strong and birthing an end-time Prophet. I know you endured hell trying to get me into the Earth and I will be forever grateful. Thank you for your love and support.

My mother in Love, Nella Cosey. You are the best. Thank you for your wisdom.

Aunt Merl: I could write a novel on what you mean to me. Thank you for always believing in me and being present in my life. You have always encouraged me to be better and I will always give you your flowers while you are here on Earth. You are a precious ruby, and your value can't be calculated.

To my husband, Pastor Nicholas E. Cosey. Thank you for believing in me and pushing me to be better. Not allowing me to be stagnant and being my rock when my father died. I was so depressed; I would not have been able to make it without you.

To my children Gabriel (24), Heaven (23), Amyyr (21), Sarynity (18) London (15), Paris (14) Nicholas Jr. (11) and Glory (6). You all made me a better person. I would have given up a long time ago. Thank you for allowing me to grow from a young naïve Moma to a rockstar (Ma-Dukes) and Grandma.

To my Grandkids Ace James and Ayla Cy'mone; affectionally known as

Granny-Dude and Granny-Girl. I love being your granny.

My siblings, Trina, Londa, Jamiee, Jeremy, and James Jr.

Special honor to my brother James. James, your support can never be repaid. I honor you because daddy leaving left a void in my life, and you helped me through some of the worst times. My little BIG Brother.

My Nieces: Ehmani (My Boo) Freyonna, Jamila, Felicity, Kiaria, Ne-Ne, Arianna, and Jade. Nephews: Dre, Caleb, Asher, Na'Varri, Caelan.

TABLE OF CONTENT

<u>PREFACE</u>

Word to the wise is a self-help book dealing with the inner hurt we all feel sometimes. Life is a journey, but unfortunately, that journey does not always feel as calm as a stream. As an author, I desire to give you another way to look at life's difficulties. As a person, I wanted to use some of my experiences to show that we all encounter rough waters and rough terrain. Yahweh is skilled in his plans for us. If we allowed the precision of his steady hand to lead, guide, direct, and navigate us, we would find that our trials, tribulations, and disappointments are easier to overcome. This book is inspired by the leading of the Holy Spirit and the breath of life He has breathed onto the pages. This book was written to encourage you that no matter what point you are in your life and what you are facing, that life is worth living and it truly gets better. Every person walking this Earth or going home to be with the Lord that experienced greatness had to overcome much before they got there! Pain is the conditioning of greatness. No pain, no gain.

Chapter 1:

Let Freedom Ring

Word to the wise: Have you ever experienced a place in your walk with God where it seemed as if there was nothing but endless valleys, constant despair, desperation, and chronic pain? Allow me to minister to you that I have been to that place, and I will be the first to tell you that it is uncomfortable. Sometimes God allows us to experience areas of pain and discomfort to mature us. If you are reading this book, then you are looking for an answer to life's difficulties. Unfortunately, each of us has an individual path to greatness; our parents cannot take our pain away from us. Our pastors cannot go through our valleys for us. Our spouses can do nothing to ensure that we will not experience any pain in our lives. The only hope that we have is in the living Word. Jesus himself.

When I came to the Father, I was broken, battered, and bruised from life's traumas and the hurts I experienced in the church. However, there was something so tranquil about coming to the Father with my torn-up self. He did not judge me, cast me away, abandon me, or criticize me. In fact, out of all the countless things I have shared with the Master, He has never repeated it to a soul. I want to encourage you that if you are feeling like your back is up against the wall, you cannot seem to get life together, cannot shake the feeling of guilt you have for allowing yourself to get finessed like you have, and you need an out, to let freedom ring.

You may be wondering, how can I let freedom ring? I am in so much bondage Sis. You do not understand. I have been this way for fifteen years. I am a whole mess out here in these streets. God does not want me. He will not even look upon me. I have entertained so much sin. Some things I cannot even tell anyone because they would be utterly disgusted. I want to be free, but I have been bound for so long that I do not have the slightest clue what freedom looks like. Would you allow me to minister to you that you are in the perfect posture for deliverance? If you are going to be free, you must first admit that you are bound. The Father views us from the inside out. We cannot lie to Him. He is all-seeing, all-knowing, all-powerful, the only wise, true and living God, and we cannot hide from Him.

Do you not know that He is the creator, and you are the creation? When baking a cake, because you are the baker and it is not store bought, you know everything in the cake. No one can try to add an ingredient to a cake you baked just like the Father created you. He knows all about you. He knows what your infirmities are. He knows what makes you angry. He knows who you do not like. He knows what irritates you. He knows how you cry at night. He knows that you harbor unforgiveness and why you are still holding on to it. He knows what a dirty uncle did to you. He knows that you do not trust people because you have been betrayed several times. God knows you better than you know yourself. You cannot hide from His all-seeing eyes, so if you are going to be free and let freedom ring, you must first confess what you have bound.

We must come to the true realization of what has kept us bound in life. In my life, I was always running from God and searching for something else to fill this ever-standing void that I have had since childhood. I was a peculiar child and I have always talked to God and He has always talked back to me.

<u>Chapter 2:</u>

The Spirit of Boo

Word to the wise: I have always wondered why some of us hop into relationships with these no-good brothers. They do not mean you any good, and the bad ones have the spirit of a finesser. Well, Sister Pastor, I really need you to break down Boo because I do not know if I have encountered him before or am dealing with him now. Boo is a proud spirit. He thrives on usury, cheating, lying, manipulation, control, dominance, narcissism, and anger. He or she is emotionally abusive, unstable, overconfident, and cunning. Most of us that have been in a meaningful relationship has encountered this spirit.

I remember being a single woman. I had my own vehicle, house, bank account and a respectable job. I had three children by the time I was 21 years of age. I was suffering from a spirit of abandonment because my children's fathers, yes, I said fathers, knocked me up and left me with the responsibility of taking care of them alone. I was beautiful, intelligent, and in church. The problem was having three children with different fathers made me an easy target for manipulation and control. It was like I had a sign on my forehead that said, date me and I will give you all my money. It is funny now that I am over that trauma from that period, but it was not funny at the time.

I had already been finessed by brothers who said that I was the only one in their lives. They loved me and would never hurt me yet left at the first sign of responsibility. Now, I have overcome the fact that I have children and am doing my best to raise them, but I have a problem, I desire to be in a relationship. The gentlemen that flocked to me saw a woman with low self-worth that wanted to be in a relationship so bad that she would accept anything from them. The first time I encountered Boo, he had worked his way into driving my car. It did not even dawn on me that this brother was driving my vehicle more than I was. It got so bad that people started thinking it was his car.

It started off smoothly. It began with opening the car door for me, filling it up with gas and occasionally cleaning it out. I was thinking, boy oh boy, I got myself a keeper. I was so wrong, and I could not see the set up. I did not realize he was doing these things to get me to drop my guard. To woo and sway me. To manipulate me into giving in. Instead of it being my car, it was now our car, although he paid no car payment or insurance, and what is even worse, he wanted me to do all the work but allow him to take the credit. Now Boo is driving around flossing in my car and had the audacity to get phone numbers while driving my car.

He started picking me up late from work. How can a person pick you up late from work when they do not work? What are you doing all day? The reason this behavior was allowed was because I had no idea who I was. I had no revelation of the glory that God would reveal through me. It had not dawned on me that you teach people how to treat you. That what you allow will eventually become your reality and to break the cycle of manipulation, I had to disallow it. The reality is that I had not had enough yet.

Every year around the holidays, Boo would begin cutting up. This brother was living a double life. He would start arguments with me so we could fight and then have a reason to leave and go to the other woman's house. This person had the nerve to start a war and then played the victim. He had a usury spirit. He was anointed to finesse me. Just like clockwork, he would start calling again after the holidays were over and January would roll around. He wanted to try and get a couple of months to give the appearance that we were working things out. That all was well, and we were doing so much better post-breakup. Allow me to introduce you to tax time Boo.

It is so sad that although scripture declares in Genesis 1:27, that we were made in His image and in 1 Peter 2:9, that we are a royal priesthood and a chosen generation, that we totally miss our value. Every tax year, this man was walking back into my life to try and come up off the very children he talked so bad about me having. I would give him money just so that he would not beg me to buy things when we were out shopping. I would find that while making my purchases, he would set his items on the counter so that I could pay for them and keep his money (the money I gave him) in his pocket. This is a usury spirit. A person that possesses a usury spirit does everything for their own self-advantage.

This spirit partners with manipulation to tear down your self-confidence and then drain your pocketbook. A person that operates in a spirit of usury thrives on control. The goal is to get you to feel so bad about yourself that you are free to be taken advantage of. What makes a man or a woman continue to return to this person? What power has convinced them that this is the best that they can do, that it gets no better than this, that they will change, just give it some time? If the devil can tell you a lie about yourself that you believe, he has already won half the battle.

<u>Chapter 3:</u>

Rejection Section

Words to the wise: Do you remember being in elementary school and you could not wait for recess? Do You remember how much confidence you had in your skills and abilities? You could not wait for break because you knew you were the fastest runner, you knew you were great at double-Dutch, you knew you were great at dodgeball, and you were confident that whoever the captains were going to be, surely, they would have to call your name and pick you because you were hot stuff. You ever notice how confident we are in our skills and abilities, who we are, what we are, and where we are going, until someone strips that from us?

Going back to recess, you are on the field, standing there with the rest of the kids, and waiting for the captain to call your name. However, they call Rachel, Tommy, Jasmine, Johnny, Patrice, Josey, Michael, and you and the little boy who always picks his nose are the last to be picked. Surely you were faster than Josey and Michael, and you know you are faster than the little nose-picker, but you were second to last. You were not aware that it was at that moment that a seed of rejection was planted, and it would be watered several times throughout your life.

If you would fess up and admit it, you were really upset that you were picked last. The reality of the matter is sometimes you are picked last and rejected due to jealousy. You knew you were the best runner until someone told you that you were not. You knew you were beautiful until someone called you ugly. You knew God called you to preach until somebody convinced you that He did not. Can I minister to you that sometimes the very person that can create a platform for you is so intimidated by who you are and what you are called to do that they will not pick you to be on their team?

Revisit the playground of your life, look at who the captain is, and open your eyes. Sometimes the captain is your boss that can promote you to the next level, but because they know that you are a self-starter and get along well with your peers, they become intimidated. The spirit of intimidation will cause them to keep your plane grounded and never allow you to go higher. Sometimes your family members are the people that try to keep you tied to the shore and anchored to your past life. They will never see you beyond the person that used to smoke and drink. They will never acknowledge the fact that God has matured you and crushed you to get the oil out of your life. They will never recognize that you no longer use your hands to fight, but now you lift them in worship to a Holy God who sanctified and delivered you.

Those who reject your gift have kept you tied to the shore because you have the same face. Our facial features do not change. Yes, we have gotten older and wiser, but if you have not had plastic surgery, you still look the same. You still look like the single woman who had all those children with different fathers. You still look like the person that would curse someone out and ask questions later. You still look like the one that used to boost clothes and sell hot items. You still look like the one that got arrested for having sticky fingers. Beloved, your face has not changed and for that reason, it is hard for some people in your life to be convinced that you have changed, reformed, and taken out a new lease on life, etc.

Would you allow me to minister to you that you will only be as great as what you are able to overcome? Sure, they rejected you and tossed you to the side as if you held no value. I understand that they talked about you like a dog and because you are radical for Christ, they labeled you a witch, called you a Jezebel, and tried their best to ruin your image with others who viewed you in a favorable light. They tried their best to kill your spiritual baby. However, if I may interject here, amid your hurt and the unforgiveness you hold based on how others have treated you, I prophesy that what God is doing for you in this season is greater than anyone's opinion of you. You will be great. You shall make power moves and you shall walk out your purpose.

Rejection will cause you to compete to be the greatest person in the room. The reason being is because others have gone so far to smother the gift, you go to unhealthy lengths to make yourself relevant. If someone is singing a song, you will make statements that you can sing it better. If they have a business, you will make comparisons regarding your business. The spirit of rejection will cause you to have an unhealthy outlook on life and people if you do not get delivered. Rejection will cause you to fall out with everyone seeking to be in a relationship with you because when you have been rejected, it is challenging to receive love from anyone. You feel as though you do not deserve love and if you accept love, that person is only showing it with an ulterior motive in mind.

Rejection will cause you to handle people with a long-handled spoon as my grandmother would call it. In the back of your mind, you have an expectation that people will snake you, sabotage you, and stab you, so when they finally commit the offense, it does not deal you the same blow because you were expecting them to do you wrong. On the flipside, if you let your guard down and allowed people to come in and then they snaked you, sabotaged you, and stabbed you, the knife wound would be deeper because you allowed them into the inner courts of your heart. But let me declare to you today that we bind the spirit of rejection in the name of Jesus. I declare and decree that you shall be free from that pit so that you can walk in victory and not offense.

Rejection will cause you to be on an island all by yourself. This spirit is so prevalent because many people wrestle with it but are living their lives as if they are okay. However, because they have been rejected and counted out, they are walking around with the spirit of offense, and because offense has been summoned by rejection, anger has been summoned by the spirit of offense. They have partnered together to ruin your life. You are offended because you know what God said and you feel as if you are being put on the back burner. They will not allow you to sing your song, will not allow you to pray, will not show up to anything you invite them to and now there is a wound of affliction. Now you are walking in offense because you are offended. They go to everybody else's events but will not show up to mine. I invited them several times, yet they always have an excuse and now that offense has reared its ugly head, here comes anger. Now you are in your flesh because you were rejected but then became offended, and then you got angry. God is calling you to greater Sis and Bro. You do not have to walk in offense or anger. Even Jesus was not received in his own environment. Sometimes you need to get away from those that have become too familiar with your anointing. You can be a Pastor and they will still call you by your first name without putting a handle on it but will not call their doctor Mike. They will call him Dr. Mike. They will call a judge, your honor and a police officer, officer such and such, but they refuse to put a handle on your appointed office. You teach people how to treat you. We cannot continue to complain about what we allow.

Chapter 4:

When Snakes Attack

Words to the wise: A familiar culprit that keeps you tied to the shore is the endless snakes in your life. I know, I know, they are your friend, a family member, you assumed that blood was thicker than water, they attend your church, your children play together, or you have known them for years, and because you are familiar with this individual or individuals, you did not have on any protective gear. You were not wearing your PPE or personal protection equipment. You did not have your Ephesians 6:33 armor on, and you thought you were good because you knew them.

Can I minister to you that those closest to you will snake you? In this COVID-19 epidemic, you cannot play any games. Everyone needs a mask on. I do not care if you are a brother, sister, friend, or foe; if you are coming to my home with my husband and children here, you need a mask. They may say they do not have the coronavirus, but we do not know if we cannot test them or if they do not have a negative result to show us, so our guards are always up. You do not do this to be rude; you do this to be safe.

Unfortunately, as believers, we must always keep our guard up because we do not know who will snake us. The devil is a wise old serpent. His tricks are ancient, and he perfects his tactics on the saints. The devil will use your cat, dog, child, your mother, your father, sister, and brother; he does not care who or what he uses to knock you off your square. The devil is an expert manipulator and sends his snakes into your life to suck your life out and spread their venom in you. His goal is to make you sick so that you will never enter the promised land. Your toes will never touch the sands of destiny. Your hair will never blow in the wind at a place called Free.

The garden snake

The garden snake is the snake that your elementary class kept as a pet. Everybody got a chance to hold this snake. It could not hurt you, but you had the power to hurt it. It slithered like a snake, hissed like a snake, had eyes like a snake, a split tongue like a snake, and you did not doubt for one minute that it was a snake. You underestimated it because it seemed harmless, but what you did not realize was that a snake is still a snake. It may have been harmless, but it still hailed from a family of snakes. You thought they were your friend and your partner, but then what you shared with them in secret when the two of you had a disagreement, they shared your innermost thoughts to hurt you, to ruin your credibility with others, and to jeopardize your reputation and your character. Yes, you trusted them because although they have snaked on you before, you all are friends, surely, they would never do it again. The Word of God commands us to forgive our brethren 70 times 7 times, but he did not tell you to lie there and continue to get bit. You can forgive those who have snaked you, but you need to be mindful to look after yourself and not continue to put yourself back in the snake pit to continue being bitten.

The Venomous Viper

This snake is deadly. In the natural world, if it bites you without any antivenom, you are most certainly going home to be with the Lord. You did not realize how deadly their bite was until you got bitten. You did not know that they despised you so much that they would call CPS on you and attempt to have your children removed from your custody. They would go on to do everything in their power to make your life a living hell. They would mention your name in every conversation that they have with a negative connotation, all with the goal of killing your ministry. The Word of God promises us in Isaiah 54:17, that no weapon that is formed against us shall prosper. You must read the Word and watch what the Father says. He says no weapon is formed, meaning that there will be weapons that are formed against us. There will be those who will lie about you, talk about you, manipulate you, and abuse you, but their weapons will not prosper in all their attempts to hurt you; their weapons will not prosper. They will not go forth. They will not accomplish what they set out to do. It's like trying to stab somebody with a butter knife; you are not going to accomplish much. Jesus told the disciples in Luke 10:19, I have given you authority to tread on snakes and scorpions and to overcome the power of the enemy, and nothing shall by any means hurt you. Jesus did not come to play around with the devil. He said nothing by any means shall hurt you. I do not care what tool or tactic the enemy has formed against you, a man of God, woman of God; it won't work and will not hurt you. You can be confident in the word of God because He is not like man that He should lie, nor the son of man that He should repent. Be free of snakes today. Stop carrying them around as if they are harmless, knowing

23

they can bite you.

The Familial Snake

For us to move forward in our lives, we must operate in true forgiveness. What is hindering us from really walking in true love and forgiveness and allowing people to be free? I get it; I am the first to admit that it is hard to forgive some snakes in your family, especially the ones that act as if they did not snake you. My mother calls it hiding your hand. I realize that blood was supposed to be thicker than water and because of what they did, you are having a tough time releasing them through forgiveness. Forgiveness is more so for you than the other party. When you forgive that person truly, you take your power back concerning the matter. The devil cannot hold it over your head that you are harboring malice. He would love nothing more than sending a spirit of unforgiveness and anger to accompany the malice lying dormant within you.

I know that there are some secrets that have trapped you since childhood because you feel as if you tell them now, you will not be believed. If you share what that uncle or that cousin, or the neighbor, or the family friend, there will be those trying to protect them and make you look like a liar or attention seeking. I know the familial snake all too well and it is never easy to deal with. You must learn to live your truth. There will be some that do not want you to share your testimony because they are in it. They had a hand in your pain and have never made amends from their wrongdoing. My sister and my brother, can I minister to you that you must be okay with the apology you will never get. It takes a humble person to apologize even if they feel that they did nothing wrong. An apology is not an admission of guilt, but it is a bridge of communication that will at least allow you and the other party to be on speaking terms. What do you mean Pastor Cosey, that an apology is not an admission of guilt? Well, I am glad you asked.

Have you ever worked in the service industry? May be a call Center, McDonalds, Burlington, Macy's, Aldo's, Wal-Mart, etc.? I do not care what service you provided for any of these vendors, but you were the face of the company, a representative to handle any matters on that company's behalf. What happens when a customer is dissatisfied? We don't send them to the corporate headquarters, but we accept responsibility and apologize that they feel that way. You are not admitting that your company did anything nefarious. However, you are acknowledging that person's feelings. As humans, it would really make our day if a person just acknowledged our feelings. It does not matter if what you are feeling is correct; merely saying that you understand where we are coming from is all that we are looking for. Beloved, I want you to forgive yourself for allowing yourself to get snaked. Next, I want to implore you to move past the pain and be okay with the apology that you may never get.

Chapter 5:

The Island of Stitches

Words to the wise: My mother has always been a very neat and tidy person. You better not leave anything laying around the house that even gave the appearance of being trash because she was throwing it away. Sometimes things that looked broken to my mother were thrown away, even though they still held value to me. I remember my Rainbow Bright doll being thrown away, probably because I had outgrown her and never played with her anymore, but that did not mean that she was not valuable to me.

As humans, we are often broken, bruised, and scarred and others have thrown us away and left us for the garbage man to pick up. However, those who threw us out did not realize that we are still valuable to God. Some of my barbie dolls were tossed out because their limbs were missing, or my brothers thought they were torpedoes. However, they could have been fixed, not trash, even though they looked broken. David was a broken man. Saul was the people's pick for King, but David was God's pick. Saul killed his thousands, but David killed his tens of thousands. David was broken but he was chosen. Let's explore.

David was not perfect. He had been anointed King and was handpicked by God. However, like Paul, he had a thorn in his flesh. He wrestled with pretty women. It was not enough for David to look at something pretty and keep his composure. David looked, became aroused, called Bathsheba to himself, laid with her although she was married, impregnated her, called her husband to him to have him go home and lay with his wife, what he did not realize was that Uriah was a man of valor and could care less about some intimacy while his soldiers were fighting at battle, and so he snaked him. He sent Uriah back to battle and put him on the front lines knowing he would be killed and when he was, he took Bathsheba to be his wife. She gave birth to their child who was a product of their adultery and sent David a message the Lord would not allow the baby to live.

Yes indeed, David was broken. He knew his heart was in trouble and he was out of the will of God. He knew he messed up and needed to rectify his ways before the Lord. He knew that his heart was wicked. How could he sleep with a man's wife, get her pregnant and then have that man killed to conceal his sin? Isn't that like us? Instead of fessing up and coming to the Lord poured out and hiding nothing, we try to conceal our sin. David knew that he was broken, and we can feel his pain and anguish in Psalm 51, where he begs God to create in him a clean heart and renew a right spirit within him.

For a heart to become clean, it must first be dirty. No one is asking for something already spotless to become clean again. In addition, David asks God to renew a right spirit within him. The word renew stands out because if God must renew a thing, he must make it like new again. In addition, David demanded the right spirit, which indicates he knew he had the wrong spirit on the inside of him.

Like David, we all have had unclean hands and need to be made clean again. God can clean us up and make us new again.

The island of stitches is for broken people. I know that people have thrown you away. They have called you a Jezebel, damaged goods, fat, ugly, bald-headed, too dark, too fat, and any other name they saw fit to call you other than what your parents named you. As a result, you have allowed that bitter seed to grow a root and fester in your life. It has grown branches around your heart and imprisoned it. Now you are an adult, stuck at the age of seven because that is the era where you were broken. Can I minister to you that God can use you in your broken state? He loves the broken. He will not throw you away or cast you asunder but receive you unto himself.

The Word of the Lord declares in Jeremiah 31: 2- 4, he says, "Yea I have loved thee with an everlasting love, therefore with lovingkindness have I drawn thee." When you are broken, you do not have to be cut open because you have already been torn, you have already been torn apart, you have already been crushed and now the great physician is ready to perform surgery. When you come to him bruised, broken, and ripped apart by life, people's words, snake bites, the Lord that great physician comes to perform heart surgery, brain surgery to renew your mind, knee surgery to install a gateway to talk to Him through prayer, back surgery to break you all the way and put you back straight, tongue surgery to remove your slick tongue and sharp words, and hand surgery to put them in a posture prayer.

Miriam-Webster defines the word stitch as a loop of thread of yarn resulting from a single pass or movement of the needle in sewing, knitting, or crocheting. It goes further to state that stitch means to make, mend, or join something with stitches (noun). When the surgeon Jesus has you open, He is removing everything that is unlike Him. Jesus came to remove all your impurities, worries, scandals, closeted items, stains of sin, sins of immorality, seeds of guilt, perversion, destruction, uncleanliness, and any other legal handles implanted by the enemy to destroy you from the inside out. After he removes that unnecessary waste, he refills you with himself. A songwriter wrote a song that said fill my cup, let it overflow, let it overflow with love. That is the true definition of a believer: there is newness.

Jesus wants to remove all our self-dependence so that we lean on Him and not our own selves. He is all-sufficient, all-knowing, and all-powerful and He knows just how to fix His creation. We have been saturated in carnality since birth. Job reminds us in Job 14, that a man that is born of a woman is on the Earth a few days and those few days are full of trouble. So, you can see the need for Jesus to get a hold of us and shake us because the reality of the matter is that we are torn up from the floor up. Romans 12: 22 reminds us not to be conformed to this world, but to be transformed by renewing our minds. So here it is that the writer is using the word "renew" again to emphasize the condition of our mind and heart.

Once Jesus performs the necessary surgery, he stitches us up. He does not allow all that goodness that He has filled us with to fall out. He also realizes that the broken can be repaired. You have not damaged goods, you are not too far gone that you are beyond fixing, and God loves you better than you can ever love yourself. If that relationship left you leaking and feeling unloved, I want to remind you that the Father loves you. If your family left you and you are wrestling with a spirit of abandonment, His word declares that He would never leave you nor forsake you. His hands can stretch the universe wide to grab you from wherever you are. We cannot hide from God. Will you allow Jesus to stitch you up today?

One of the reasons why we are so toxic is because we have not been to the surgeon to get stitched up. We are bleeding all over the place. Some of us preachers have been bleeding all over our sermons. We are not helping the people; we are really venting in "C" sharp and "B" flat and calling it a message. We are coming off angry and messy over the pulpit and we do not realize that the congregants know who you are talking about. They also know that you have not been private enough to keep some of the business. Before we minister, we ought to purify ourselves before the Lord and ask for His guidance so that our message is His message and not one of trying to get people together. Do not bleed on people. If you have ever had a nosebleed, you know that it makes an utter mess. Blood is so messy that it does not like to wash out and it ruins garments. However, the blood of Jesus will stain you and you will not want to rinse Him out. His blood never loses its power. The blood of Jesus has saving and staying power. Our blood makes a mess of things, but His blood cleans us up.

When you first get stitches, you can see them. People can see our stitches when we first come to God and are going through our transition. You can see the wound that was stitched. I remember when my son Gabriel was three years of age, and he had these pajamas with slippery feet. I told him several times to stop running because the house we resided in had hardwood floors. The combination of those pajamas and hardwood floors were not a good mix. Being three and having his own mind, Gabriel continued to run on that floor until the slippery pajamas took him for the ride of his life. He slid headfirst into the couch that had a metal piece hanging from the base of it. Needless to say, he cut his lip in half. He was not aware that his lip was dangling as he walked to me for comfort. He was in complete shock and the adrenaline he was experiencing shielded him from the pain. I called my Aunt Merl and asked her to go to the hospital with me as my son's lip was hanging off. I just knew that the hospital staff was going to judge me and remove him from my care. They probably assumed I was an unfit mother.

I was 20 years old, and he was my first child. The staff took Gabriel back and my aunt went back with us. They numbed his lip with a numbing agent and proceeded to stitch him, but he could still feel it. He told the doctors to stop cutting him. Isn't that something? My son was receiving stitches, but he felt as if he was being cut. I want to let you know that on this journey, some of your stitches will feel like cuts. You will feel like God is cutting you and it is uncomfortable. My son is 24 years of age now and there is no scarring from the stitches. However, they were in his lip for two weeks before they dissolved.

Some of your stitches are going to be the dissolving kind.

They are going to melt right in your mouth. Can I tell you that when you first get stitched that wound looks hideous, but time passes and wounds heal? God is getting ready to grant you the type of healing that leaves no traces of brokenness. You will look at yourself and say I cannot believe the work he performed. I look so new. You will go through the fire but will not smell like smoke. There will be no soot, ashes, burn marks, and no evidence that you have ever been in a fire. He will stitch you and then shine you with the refiner's fire. Do you desire to be stitched up? Can you use stitching? Have you gotten stitched by the Master and then those stitches came loose before they could set? What do you mean, Pastor? I mean, God delivered you, but you did not hold onto it. You received your deliverance from sexual immorality, but you fell into the snare of the enemy. You knew that you were not strong enough to move past the whiff of the cologne or the perfume. It was late and you did not discipline yourself and you fell into the trap. Now you need new stitches. Can I minister to you that Jesus never runs out of stitches? His supply room is stocked full of needles, thread, and bandages. He has never lost a patient and you are safe in His care.

Chapter 6:

Come and Shine Again

Word to the wise: Can you recall a time in your life when you were full of life, full of joy, happy beyond measure, you were enjoying being alive, you were at peace with where you were in your life, and you were content with who you were and where you were? Now, allow me to also ask you if you can remember what caused you to have an interruption in your peace and joy and made that place of contentment become one of resentment.

Miriam-Webster defines the word stripped as: the process of removing all coverings from a thing, to leave bare accessories and fittings, and to make bare or naked. Sometimes we go through storms in life and after you come out and the storm clouds go away and the rain dries up, you are left feeling like something was snatched from you. You feel as though someone, or something, stole from you and stripped you of what was yours. Well, if that has ever been you or you are presently stuck on Give Me Back My Joy Boulevard, allow me to welcome you. Let us walk the block and take back everything the devil has stolen.

The Word declares in John 10: 10, that the thief, speaking of Satan, cometh to do three things, kill, steal, and destroy. It's not enough for the devil to snatch what rightfully belongs to the believer, but after he steals our stuff, he then taunts us because he knows how badly we want our things back. Think about the last time somebody stole something from you. I remember having a fictitious credit card company call me and offer me a credit card. I must have had. I do not know any better written on my forehead because they played me like a sucker. They had me pay $50 for them to send me a credit card. I had never had a credit card and I did not know that card companies would require a full application before sending you a card. These people had my name and phone number and my $50. I felt violated. I could not believe that people were calling random citizens and stealing their hard-earned money. Well, believe it because the devil is an expert finesser and his con game is a mile long.

The devil has spent years breaking you down and stripping you of things that belong to you. He stripped you of your self-esteem, dignity, fire, zeal, energy, joy, money, value, and your coat of many colors. I want you to know that the devil comes to strip you to harm you, but Jesus came to strip you to restore your joy. We become dull when we return to the Lord after living any kind of way, parading around raggedy before Him, being sinful, unholy, and uncaring. The further we walk away from the light of God, the duller we become. We need to enter the refiner's fire so that we can become shiny again.

The Father strips us like a janitor strips a floor. I remember my husband working for a hospital as a floor tech. Before a floor can be stripped, the floor tech must clear the area of obstacles that will prohibit smooth stripping. What obstacles has the Lord cleared out of your pathway so that He can have you to Himself to perform His work? I remember being in a terrible relationship for 8 years. It was so toxic, and I should have run for the hills which cometh my help before I got hurt, but I did not heed the Word of the Lord or the constant warnings that He gave me, and I ended up paying for it.

This person robbed me of my self-confidence, my joy, and my value. He made me question how I felt about myself. My self-esteem was ruined. My confidence was depleted and when I finally got up the nerve to leave, he tried to trick me into staying and taunted me when I refused. I remember him finessing me out of my tax money, spending the money out of my pocket and taking it away from my children for his wants and needs. Stealing my children's WII Nintendo system that I purchased for their enjoyment. Stealing our rent money set aside for the property owner and snorting it up his nose. He cheated on me countless times and would play mind games with me by starting an argument just so he could leave. He would call me every name in the book until it became normal. He would stunt on my children in front of his friends and me by sitting in an armchair in the living room and having us serve him like he was a king. But God delivered me from that pit. I could not see that that relationship was draining me of my beauty and causing my light to become dull. I was unequally yoked and in love with a devil. The Lord delivered me, but before He could complete His work, He had to strip me Himself. The devil stripped me, and I became dull, but God came to strip me to restore my shine.

The Lord begins by clearing obstacles and removing all hindrances from you. He omits all the idols we have resurrected in place of Him. He is calling us higher. The Father is saying children come higher. I want to show you some things. He wants to get you alone so that He can work. Our jobs have become idols, our children have become idols, and our marriages have become idols; they get all our time, all our praise, and all our adoration, leaving nothing for the Father. What have you erected as an idol before your Father? He will not share his glory with another, so idols must come down. It will have a violent fall. It will crash and break.

Next, the janitor must then mix the stripper. The stripping solution must first be diluted. The Father desires to just add water. I love making pancakes, especially the kind where you only have to add water. That pancake mixture does not require anything but water before it can be cooked. Jesus comes to bring us living water. John 4:14 says," But those who drink the water I give them will never thirst again." He wants to know if you are thirsty. Some of us have been through so much that we are completely dry, withered, and worn. The Father dilutes our product; everything in us, unlike Him, must be diluted to make it weaker as He becomes stronger. Are you ready to be diluted?

The third step is to apply the stripper. The floor tech will do this by flood-mopping the area. They say that it is important not to allow the product to dry. During this process, it is also important to use a plastic bag to cover up the solution so there is no cross-contamination. What things in your life have cross-contaminated your witness? The scripture tells us in Matthew 6:24 that no man can serve two masters; either he will love one and hate the other. Do not allow yourself to be cross-contaminated in your flesh while the Lord is stripping you.

While the stripper is being applied and allowed to dwell, the tech uses a floor scrubber to scrub all the old wax off the floor. There are areas while the tech is stripping the floor that have less traffic than others such as the corners. These are the areas that contain more of the old wax. The way that a floor tech can tell if he is stripping a floor the proper way is that while he or she is scrubbing, the floor becomes dull.

The Father must take all that old wax from us. He scrubs us and removes everything that used to make you shine, but His light by itself causes us to shine. For years, I thought I was so happy in that old relationship I had a shine that was not from God. The words of people that have inflated our egos produce a haughty, prideful, and arrogant shine that is not from God. The little gods that we have erected in the Lord's place have given us a false shine. He comes to strip everything that is unlike Him so we can shine again. Life has beat us up so that some of us have completely lost any hope of our shine returning. It does not matter what we do; we still feel so unfulfilled. Allow me to prophesy to you that if you have been feeling a little dull lately, the Father has come to restore your shine. Weeping may endure for the night, but joy cometh in the morning.

The next step is to discard the remaining wax. All the leftover residue from your old shine is causing you to be dull. It is now time to ensure that you get it all and leave no remnants of the last wax job. The tech may use a squeegee or other tool to help him remove all remaining wax. They may even use a wet vac to suck up the residue from the old wax. The Father does not desire for you to bring anything old into your newness. Why do we insist on bringing old people into our new territories? It is true that when you are on your way to a land of new, some of the old things in your past cannot journey with you. He goes further to rinse off any remaining residue just to make sure that He got it all. I implore you that while you are in the process of becoming new, to not allow guilt to set in when you are forced to leave old relationships, old behaviors, and things that did not work behind. He came to make you brand new.

The tech then applies the new wax. The new shine is applied to life. You went through the process of removing obstacles, taking off the coat of old wax, scrubbing the hard areas, and rinsing to make sure there is nothing left, to now getting a fresh coat of wax. You thought that leaving that abusive relationship was going to kill you, but you were being set up for the stripping to give you a fresh coat of wax. You thought that when they talked about you, that you were going to lose your joy forever, but what you did not realize is that the Father was stripping you to give you a fresh coat of wax. You thought that when you lost everything, you were going to lose your mind, but what you were not privy to was the conversation that Jesus was having with the Father, who told the Holy Ghost to strip you and give you a new coat of wax. When you get a fresh coat of wax, there is nothing left to do but shine on the devil! What can the devil do to you? If God is for you, He is more than the world against you.

The shine always turns out dull when you buy a coat of wax from a worldly supplier. In the natural, when a floor has not been properly waxed, a white substance starts to get on the soles of shoes and the clothing of those who are passing through the area. There is a term for this. It means that the finish is literally walking. I read an article stating that a low-quality finish would oxidize because it lacked stability, and a powdery substance appears once deterioration begins to set in. When you get your wax from the world system, you get a low-quality finish, and the residue gets on anyone you touch. When you allow people to walk all over you, they destroy your finish. When you walk in constant sin, you destroy your finish and cause it to become dull. You destroy your finish when there's improper application of the Word of God in your life. The tech can use a product called Replicator. That product's function is to restore a dull floor's finish. The Holy Ghost is to the spirit what Replicator is to the natural. The Holy Ghost comes to restore your finish. The Holy Spirit is our paraclete which is Greek for our advocate or helper. He's our comforter. He helps us to produce fruit. He produces a change in us and causes us to have a balanced approach to life. When we have a new finish, we treat people better, our mouths are not as slick, we are nicer to those close to us, and we are pleasant to be around. He does not strip us to make us bitter, but He strips used to make us better.

The Father needed to give you a new finish because you were dull. Your spiritual tree was not producing fruit. Harvest time was coming and going year after year and there was no evidence that our trees were even fruit trees. They were planted and erect, but nothing was growing. Have you ever been in a season where you felt stagnant and stuck, like you were not growing, and you could not figure out why you were not growing? If you are reading this and are in a dull and desolate season, we bind stagnation in the name of Jesus. We stimulate your spiritual growth and declare and decree that this is the last season that harvest will come around and you produce no fruit.

Galatians 5: 22 states, "But the fruit of the Spirit is love, joy, peace, forbearance, kindness, goodness, faithfulness, gentleness, and self-control. Against such, there is no law." You, my brother, and my sister are getting ready to shine bright like a diamond. You are going to have a finish with extra gloss. Why? Because your fruit tree is in full bloom. You do not even get mad when they do you wrong anymore and instead of going off, you pray for them. You do not even get upset when they work your patience and take your kindness for weakness. Instead, you have pity on them because the Holy Spirit has caused you to love your enemies instead of seeking revenge.

Paul can be a witness for us that for him to keep his finish shiny and not dull, he had to die daily. (Luke 9:23) It is true that something must die for us to truly live. Jesus declares in John 11:25, "I am the resurrection and the life, whoever believes in me, though he dies, yet he shall live." He is the only way for us to truly live, which is why he died for our sins. Paul was bearing witness to us that we must die daily to keep this glossy finish. Every day something within us that is living and stinking need to be killed and buried. Our stinking thinking needs to die. Our malicious ways need to die. The new finish is resemblant of a new man. The old man with the dull finish has been buried and needs to remain that way. A dead man has no rights nor any personal agenda. He Has nowhere to be, no more purpose, no goals, no ambitions, and he is not tempted to error before the Lord because he is deceased. The new man is living, breathing, and has a fresh finish. His steps are being ordered by the Lord. He has a destiny. He has goals and dreams and when he accepted the Lord Jesus Christ in his heart, he was gifted with the Parakletos to walk beside him to advocate for him. It's because of this new mindset that there is no longer room for the old man's ambitions and fleshly desires. He has had his turn to wreak havoc in your life, but you have become stripped, buffed, and waxed. Do not allow the old man to walk on and deteriorate your new coat of wax. Shine on the devil because you are new again.

Chapter 7:

Life is like a game of spades.

Words to the Wise: One of my favorite movies is Forrest Gump. There are so many life lessons in that one movie. One of my favorite lines is when he is sitting at the bus stop, which he is doing for 75% of the movie, and he offers the lady sitting beside him some of the chocolates that he was bringing to Jenny for a gift. He tells her that life is like a box of chocolates; you never know what you are going to get. The Holy Spirit dropped this revelation in my spirit. He said, "Daughter, this phrase is key because he was making inference that life is an assortment of obstacles, and you never know which one you are going to experience until you are forced to taste it.

This revelation is so prevalent because no one knows what is beyond the chocolate covering and hiding in the middle. The middle flavors are sometimes coconut, lemon, cherry, and creme. The one thing that is consistent is the milk chocolate. Sometimes you bite into a flavor that is not your cup of tea. The result is that you take a bite and throw away the rest. To be honest, had you known that the center of the chocolate-covered piece was coconut, you would not have eaten it to begin with. Now, one hour and a swollen lip later, you are dealing with the effects of something that looked good to you and was appealing to the eye, but the result was that it was not good for you.

You also learned a valuable lesson about reading the ingredients before eating something you are allergic to. You learned quickly that eating the unknown had the potential to do you real bad out here in these streets. For some of us, our eyes can be swollen shut from eating the wrong thing and you still take part of that which did you more harm than good. Yes, there is revelation in watching Forrest Gump. The moral of this story is that everything that looks good and tastes good may not be good for you. But I am reminded of the Word of God in Psalm 34:8, which declares, O taste and see that the Lord is good.

Dealing the cards

Forrest stated that life was like a box of chocolates, but I beg to differ. I am smooth off 10th and Burleigh and life is just like a hood game of Spades. Now I would like to test my audience here because you are only going to understand this analogy if you are a spade player. Well preacher, how do I know if I'm a real spade player? You are not a real spade player if you don't know how to read your partner's body language. Suppose you don't recognize that if your partner is throwing off so that you can cut, you are not a real spades player. If you do not know how to bid your hand, you are not a real spades player. Lastly, because these should be enough, if you are constantly reneging and costing you and your partner three books a whop, you don't need to ever touch the cards until you learn some manners. I am just kidding, but I am serious about the spade game because I come from a spade-playing family.

The Father comes to heal our brokenness and throughout our lifetime, there have been several things that have broken us. For this reason, a lot of us are walking around bitter and broken and left in a stagnant position because we are carrying the weight of what has happened to us. God does not want us to be bitter concerning the cards we were dealt in life. Just like the game of spades, no player has control of the cards he or she is being dealt. Some of my aunts and uncles refuse to look at their cards until the dealer is done dealing because they do not want to be mad early. Some people look at their partners like they have lost their minds because surely your partner would not deal you a bunch of mess. The reality is when you finally look at your hand, you ask yourself, who dealt this mess? It is really a rhetorical question because we know exactly who dealt this mess because we watched them deal with it. The logical explanation says the dealer has no control of what you are dealt unless the joker fixed the game.

The Big Joker Anointing

There are times in our life that we go through things and our backs are up against the wall. We have prayed, fasted, and danced on it and just when you think the devil is setting you up for immediate defeat, the Lord comes through. Isn't that just like the game of spades? You are sitting there with all these cards you have been dealt with. You and your partner are trying your best not to get set and you told them you had at least one book. The problem is that your partner is fresh out of spades and cannot help you. He does not even have a possible left and it looks like you all are about to get up from the table. What your opponents nor your partner knew was that when they threw out that Ace of Spade and started dancing because they forgot there was one card that had not been played yet, you were sitting over there cool as a cucumber, waiting for them to finish their victory laps and then they realize you hadn't played your card yet. Then the moment of truth arrives and when they all look up and come to, you have the big joker stuck to your forehead like now what? What is the devil going to do with that big joker? Let me prophesy to you that the Lord has given you a big joker anointing in this season. There is no weapon that can match a card that is higher than every card. The name of the Lord Is higher than every name. He is the greatest power source; no light is greater than His light.

That's a Bad Jack

There are times when you are playing spades that the dealer doesn't deal you anything you can use. None of the cards he has sent your way will even be a threat to the enemy. In addition, you know that this will be one round that you will just have to survive because you have nothing to fight with in your arsenal. You and your partner have been getting assaulted the whole round. It almost looks like the other team is getting ready to run on Boston on yall. You are about to get set and it is not going to be pretty. You are thinking to yourself that you all went board because you did not have anything and now it looks like a jack is about to seal the deal. What happened? How did this hand come down to this? It is the last hand of the game; your opponents have nine books; you and your partner have three. You need one more book to make.

You know what you have in your hand, and it is not looking pretty. The first team threw out three clubs, your partner threw out ten hearts, and then the other team threw out a jack of clubs and started dancing. They start high-fiving each other and screaming set, yall set. Somebody even started shouting as if they were at the church, but then your reaction was not the reaction of a person who just got set. There was not any disappointment on your face. You did not make any motions as if you were getting ready to get up. But when they looked at you, you were pointing to your forehead. There was a deuce of spades stuck to your forehead. Do you know how bad they looked after all that running, all that taunting and talking slick, and the whole time you had a deuce of spades?

Isn't that what life is like? I said do you play spades? Are you a real spade player? Just when the devil thought he had you, the Lord visited you with a deuce anointing. In the nick of time, when you were getting ready to lose it. The repo man showed up at your job and took your car. You were embarrassed because all your co-workers knew it was your vehicle. The devil thought taking your car was going to break you, but the deuce came to save the day. People talked about you so badly that you were ready to cut everybody off, oh but the deuce anointing. It does not matter how the devil lied to you and told you that you were trapped and said there was no escape for you. The deuce anointing brings credence to 1 Corinthians 10:13, "There hath no temptation taken you, but such as is common to man; but God is faithful who will not suffer you to be tempted above that ye are able; but will with the temptation also make a way to escape, that ye may be able to bare it.

God has already given you a pathway to escape from the devil's attacks. I know that having the deuce does not always feed well in spades because you want to win with a bang instead of narrowly staying in the game. Would you allow me to minister to you just to stay in the race? Do not waive the white banner, do not speak defeat with your mouth, do not lay down and die. You've got the victory. Lift your head because you made it to another round. And guess what, that may have been a terrible round, but the dealer has got to deal again. Psalm 3:3, but thou, O Lord, art a shield for me, my glory, and the lifter of mine head. Lift up your heads, O ye gates, and be ye lifted up ye everlasting doors and the King of Glory shall come in. Who is this King of glory? The LORD of hosts, He is the King of glory. God has already done it for you. He is the king of glory.

45

The Trump Tight anointing

Word to the wise, there is a time when the dealer deals that the hand you get is unfair for everybody, including your partner. As you pick those cards up one by one, you already know that it is an absolute wrap for the other team. Their feelings are getting ready to be hurt the minute they put out something you do not have early in the game. Simply because the dealer did not give you any of them at all. You have no hearts, no clubs, two diamonds which are an Ace and the King of diamonds, and the rest are all spades. You, my friend, are Trump-tight, and you are getting ready to run those spades simultaneously by pulling the opponent's weapons. You are running so many spades that by the time they get to the one diamond that would have cut, they are forced to throw off because they have nothing else in their arsenal to cut with. Ha, ha devil you lose again.

Everything is thrown at you in the trump tight season you will cut immediately. We do not argue with demons and negotiate them coming out; we command them to come out because we are trump tight. When you are trump tight, when it is your turn, you control the board, and nobody can get a turn because you are racking up books. Sometimes your partner can get in and score a few books, and when the opponent tries to cut your partner's book, you light him up. Can I prophesy that you are trump tight as a believer? Isaiah 54: 17 declares. "No weapon that is formed against me shall prosper, and thou shalt condemn every tongue that shall rise against thee in judgment. There is nothing the devil can do when you are trump tight. He may throw his card out, but you are going to end up with the book. No weapon, no spade you throw can touch a spade that I have in my arsenal. Just because the devil formed the weapon, does not mean it is going to work.

Because you are wearing your Ephesians 6: 11, armor, the devil could not penetrate the force field of protection that was around you. Now you cannot play your opponent's hand for them. You also cannot use the weapons in their hand to help yourself win. Likewise, we cannot use the devil's weaponry for our spiritual battle. We cannot use carnal weapons to help us win a spiritual war. You cannot be spiritual and still curse folks out. We cannot be spiritual; the first time something makes us upset, we go for the jugular.

The Word declares in Ephesians 6:12, For we wrestle not against flesh and blood, but against the rulers, against the authorities, against the cosmic powers over this present darkness, against the spiritual forces of evil in the heavenly places. Romans 8:31, says, "If God be for us, who can be against us?" David said in Psalm 144, "Blessed be the Lord, my rock, who trains my hands for war, and my fingers for battle. He went further in Psalm 18: 34 and stated, "He trains my hands to war, so that my arms can bend a bow of bronze. "Make no mistake about it; every situation you go through is training you for battle. God is teaching your hands to war. Do not despise the cards you have been dealt in life because the dealer must deal again and now your trump tight.

<u>Chapter 8:</u>

Like the Dew in the Morning

Word to the wise: Chapter 8 is a hard chapter for me to write because it will be one of the more transparent chapters of my life. Some things I say may offend some people, but I must speak the truth to help someone else. Chapter 8 is where I will walk through my testimony. The number eight is only fitting because it is not meant to offend, but it is meant to highlight the grace of God that is in my life and the new beginning that God gave me.

Allow me to first apologize to those whom this chapter may offend. Because love covers a multitude of faults, I will not share names nor direct association, but because it cost me something, I have every right to write what I have been through because I have earned it with my tears. Again, this is not to point fingers or pass the blame around. I believe in order for an individual to be well rounded; they must first understand who they are to determine why they are the way that they are.

I called Chapter 8 like the dew in the morning because as a little girl, I used to rise early on Saturday mornings when I did not have school and stare out the window. It would be so warm in the house, but you could tell that it was very cool outside. I used to watch the sun peek through the trees and as it would hit the leaves. You could behold the dew of the morning resting on the trees. I have always loved the morning because I was a peculiar child. I would lay there and ask God questions and think about my future and what I desired to become. While most children would dream of becoming doctors and lawyers, even police officers, women, or firefighters. That was not my destiny. I desired to be a writer. I loved Langston Hughes and thought to myself because I did not know better that he was my idol at the time.

I loved the morning because there were no arguments in the morning. In the morning, yesterday's mess was put to bed the night before. It was quiet in the morning and free from drama. In the morning, I had time to myself to think freely and to be left alone. As I watched those droplets of condensation rest on the leaves of trees, I thought to myself, "It didn't rain last night; how did God water the morning without any rain?" Then He would reveal to my spirit that, daughter this is a new mercy. I make everything new in the morning. That is why I have always appreciated Psalm 30:5 that indicates that weeping may endure for the night, but joy cometh in the morning.

A lover of Al Green, I have always desired to meet him sometime in this lifetime. He has gotten me through so many tough times in my life. When my soul was aching from the hurtful words that people said to me, or the way that I was treated, even in my circle, Al Green would sooth my soul like David did for Saul. I remember a period of time in my late teens, having two children and overhearing a conversation about not allowing me to wear my sister's clothing because they did not know where I had been, almost calling me a whore behind my back. I felt like they were poisoning the way that my sister thought, like I was some kind of streetwalker. I do not care if I was promiscuous or if I even looked like a streetwalker; that leaves a mark on a person, especially when you are saying it behind their back instead of to their face. In addition, we wore each other's things, so she did not feel that way before she was told by others, and it conditioned her heart against me. That is why it is so important for us not to try to poison people against a person just because you feel a certain kind of way. You are inviting them to sin. The bible declares if you have an ought with your brother, you take it to them and not to any and everybody who will listen.

I remember being so heartbroken because I have always had this stigma on me of too many kids or people talking about me to those I had influence with to give me a bad rap and take the smile off my face. I went from being the nice Kisha to the one whose heart was stoney because those who I would do anything for, that were my people, would sit in groups and discuss me for hours as if they were perfect. The devil spoke to me in my bedroom on 24th and Townsend and said, "Why don't you drive your car into a tree and kill yourself? Your mom can take the kids; they will be better off without you. They will miss you when you are gone. "It sounded like a great idea. My soul was vexed, my spirit was wounded, and I truly did not desire to live. I just wanted to escape. I have been talking to the Lord since I was 2 years old. I knew He would never treat me like that, and I just really desired to be where He was.

The Holy Spirit ministered to me at once and said, "No, daughter." This is not the way. I sat in that room, bawling my eyes out. I was a complete wreck. I could not pack up my things and leave because I was 19 years of age with two babies and had nowhere else to go. I believe that some of us are not as far as we could be in life because of all the negative words planted in us and watered with jealousy and envy. Had we been treated better and had life spoken into us, we would be a lot farther. Some children need validation. They need to hear that you love them, that you are proud of them, that they did an excellent job, that they are the best at whatever they are showing interest in, that they can do whatever they want to do if they can speak it and trust God. However, many of us are forced to speak this to ourselves and once we respect numero uno, everyone else respects us too.

Can I prophesy to someone reading this book that is saying, "Pastor Cosey, that's really not that bad; my family has done worse." I am not finished just yet, beloved. Can I testify? I was pregnant with my son Nicholas. I had an issue with vomiting my entire pregnancy. It was this pregnancy that did my teeth in. The acid that constantly came up from my stomach had completely eroded my top layer of teeth. My potassium was so low that my heartbeat had become irregular. My husband was getting constant calls to come and pick me up from work because I was getting sick and vomiting every lunch hour in the parking lot. I had gone to the hospital so much that the last time I went, the doctor told me at 7 months pregnant, I was under weight. He said Mrs. Cosey, "If you come back again for vomiting, we'll have to keep you for observation and find out why you can't keep anything down." That was Monday of that week. The next day, I went to lunch with my girlfriend Tracy; I vomited so badly I could not catch my breath. My husband was called again. He picked me up and because of what the doctor said the day before, I shared with him that I knew they were going to admit me, so we'd better go to the grocery store now. We went and spent about $200 in groceries. We needed to have something in the refrigerator that the kids could make on their own without having to cook a huge meal. I knew he was going to be going back and forth.

We got all kinds of things like pizzas, noodles, hot pockets, French fries, pizza rolls, etc., so that they could have something quick to eat. As planned, I said goodbye to my kids and went to the emergency room. The doctors gave me a cracker and a 7-Up to see if I could keep them down. It did not work. I threw them right up, and that was it. I was being admitted. I would be in that hospital for 7 days on a combination of drugs, one being Reglan which was supposed to help with nausea. It made me feel worse. I was anxious and shaking. I felt like I could not sit still and was so sad. When my kids came to see me, I was depressed when they were leaving. I was so lonely in the hospital that I had a breakdown when they left. I knew my husband could not stay because he had to tend to the house. Our kids at the time were 15, 14, 11, 8, 5, and 3.

While in the hospital, my husband received several phone calls ripping him a new one for leaving the kids alone and visiting me at the hospital. Understand that the eldest was 15 and some of those days, they did not want to come. We had asked my eldest sister to assist us while I was in the hospital. My husband was told that I was in the best possible care, but they never came to see me. I was feeling some type of way because there was no way any of my family could be in the hospital and sick to that magnitude without me coming to check on them, especially their kids. That was not the worst part. While my husband was visiting on the fourth day of my being admitted, I received a call from Child Protective Services that my children were alone in the house with nothing to eat. Nothing could be further from the truth.

This is what the allegation was. However, she soon found out that that was a lie in my Maury voice. She visited the kids at school. They were clean, happy, healthy and confirmed that they were not being left alone. Dad also brought them to the hospital to visit as well. What was hurtful is that it was my own family that called CPS on me instead of coming themselves. This was done to hurt me because how can you make it better when a person is in the hospital? They are already sick; now they must fight not to lose their kids because of an allegation. This is the worst betrayal that I have ever been through in my life. I had snake bites all over my back and it was from the garden snakes who I thought were harmless. I thought to myself, Nekisha, they have not always treated you the best, but they will not try to hurt you maliciously. I never got an apology for that. I would never do my own like that and still to this day, I cannot fathom why anyone would do that to someone they say they love.

But God! It is the Holy Spirit that gives a forgiving spirit and allows us to move past our worst pain. What the devil did not realize was that God was allowing me to be crushed for the next wave of glory that was getting ready to hit my life. He allowed me to be ostracized, talked about, uninvited when everyone else was invited, ridiculed and stepped on so that His glory could shine through me. What the devil does not realize is that when people are pressing you and sucking the life out of you, they are pushing you closer to God. It was at that moment that I cried so much I had to fall on my face and scream loud enough for the Father to hear me. He touched me, healed my broken heart, and mended the relationships. Most people that got snaked to that magnitude would never speak to their family again. They would never go to another family function. They would write them completely off and act as if they did not exist but God. The Father turned my heart soft and reminded me that I must be willing to forgive what is unforgivable for me to walk with Him. It is easy to forgive something that did not hurt you, but can you forgive that which broke you?

I know pain all too well. So much that I have built up a tolerance for pain. So, you are experiencing a valley in your life. Can you forgive that which is unforgivable? Can you forgive that cheating husband that cheated on you emotionally by way of pictures and texts, fantasizing about the next woman while being married to you? Can you let it go and cast it into the sea of forgiveness? Can you forgive the foul names you were called during an intense argument? Can you forgive them for cursing you smooth out and not apologizing but acting as if it never happened and now you have internalized those words? I want to know if you can forgive it all so you can move forward and live.

Can you discipline your tongue to not speak when you want to say something? Can you discipline your flesh to not seek revenge when you have been done bad out here in these streets? Can you still be cordial and have genuine love in your heart when you are in a den of snakes? It will be bittersweet if you are still and allow God to exact His revenge. Don't you know that God can get folks better than we ever could? He will trouble them in their sleep with conviction concerning what they did to you, but if you seek your own revenge, He cannot because you have already done it. Two objects cannot share the same space. We cannot change adults; the Holy Spirit must move on their heart to change it.

What I learned over time and from falling, face planting so many times, is that instead of snitching to God on everybody else and what they did to me, I had to snitch on myself and ask God to change me. He does not take too kindly to us trying to sic him on his other children like he is a Pitbull or something. God is no respecter of persons. He reigns over the just as well as the unjust. When we go to God with our complaints, the goal should be God work on me. Search me deep and wide, and if you find anything that is unlike you, remove it all, including the root, so it can never grow back.

Chapter 9: The Box

Word to the wise: Oftentimes, God has so much in store for us that we almost feel undeserving of that place or that promotion. It is true that the scripture reveals that even at our best, we are filthy rags, and no good thing lies within our flesh, but He desires to take us to a place in Him that will blow our minds.

There are times along this journey when the Father will send a season of elevation into our lives and a fresh wind of revelation in His Word that will take us to higher heights and deeper depths, but somehow, we do not feel as though we belong there. In an earlier chapter, we discussed those anchors that have kept us tied to the shore. In this chapter, I'd like to discuss the box people put us in and the lid they put on top of it.

The box signifies a certain season or place that we have been in for a certain period of time. The box is a stagnant place, a place where triumph has passed many times. In the box, you can only stretch as wide as the box is. There is no room for growth in the box. You can outgrow the box, but the box cannot outgrow you. The reality of the matter is that some of our boxes are too small to house our anointings and we are bursting at the seams.

I remember purchasing my husband and my sons some sweaters and shirts for Christmas this past year. I purchased some boxes from Wal-Mart to wrap the gifts in. In the package, there were several boxes. There were some that were large shirt boxes; there were medium-sized boxes, and some boxes that were small like the one you would use for smaller clothing items like a scarf or a pair of socks.

I guess I did not realize how many sweaters and sweatshirts I had purchased. I used all the bigger boxes needed to wrap the bulky items. What I did next was trying to put one of the sweatshirts into a medium sized box, but it didn't go over too well. That box was too small for that sweatshirt, but laziness kicked in and I did not want to fight the holiday lines just to purchase more boxes. I did everything in my power to get that shirt to fit in the box.

I laid on the box while my daughter Ryni tried to tape it back. I taped one side down, then tried to close the side and push the other side down to attempt to tape that side, but it didn't work. I put so much effort into trying to put something too big in a box too small I was exhausted. What am I saying to you today, my brother and my sister? What God has put on the inside of you is bigger than the small minute box people have tried to force you into. You have been losing friends, family members have stated that you are doing too much, and they say that you are extra all because the box they tried to package your anointing in is too small to house the anointing on the inside of you.

There is a box entitled Joseph; you did not have that dream; and if you did, you're interpreting it the wrong way. The preacher you saw was not you; you were the singer. The great prominent preacher that you saw was your brother. He is the one with the gift. He's The one that will make it in life. He's The one that will be the greatest in the family. No, Joseph you didn't dream that God didn't show you that; you're not going to get that promotion; you can't do that job, Joseph. So, they will put you in that box, squish you in it and tie a bow around you to solidify that they do not expect you to grow anymore. Sometimes the negative word of a witch will cause you to stay in that box and be afraid to grow out of it because of the word that has been spoken against you. You will stop trying to exceed that box and stay right where a person's mouth has put you. This box is equivalent to a person catching the bus with a driver's license in their pocket. This box will have a person with a master's degree in accounting working at Burger King because they are too afraid to work in their area of expertise.

What Box have people put you in? I remember being in a season when the Father was really maturing my preaching ministry. He would give me revelation knowledge like I could not believe. In addition, the prophetic faucet was flowing with crystal clear water, and I could hear God so clearly. God was really blessing me and using me, and I was so humbled because of it. I remember getting calls to MC programs all the time. They wanted me to come, exhort and bind devils and work hard to make the program easier for the speaker when they got up. The goal was to kill two birds with one stone. Have a great preacher and a great mc and only must give one an honorarium. It is sad because I did not preach for money, but I always gave preachers the same respect that I desired in return. The moral of that story is that if you continue to only allow yourself to be seen and utilized as an MC, you will never have the respect of a studied preacher. They will always invite you to MC or to come to the service, but you will never be the main speaker.

That box has been a pinnacle of strength for some of us. We have gotten so accustomed to the box that we have painted the walls, put up a fence around it, hung pictures, put up decorative floral arrangements, and laid new flooring. We have made that once uncomfortable box comfortable for us to stay in, to lay dormant in, and to become stagnant in. You have been wondering why you have no desire to lift the lid off the box and move out of it. The box has become your best friend. You can tell it all your secrets; it knows your faults, and it knows that as long as you have decorated the interior, you will never leave. Even when you try to step out and do massive things, the moment you are rejected, you run back to that box for safety.

Would you allow me to prophesy to you that this box has crippled your destiny? This box is a crutch because its roots are grounded in fear. That box has long roots. The only reason someone was able to put you in it and scare you into never leaving it is because it is rooted in fear. This spirit has been lying dormant. As soon as you moved in, it stopped by and became a co-tenant with you. Fear moved right in and said I would like to sign the longest lease that is possible. Fear has literally kept some of us hostage. It has cost us countless opportunities.

After fear moved in the box, so did rejection. Rejection and fear are best friends. Now when you are offered opportunities, fear says, "Don›t step out and do that; it is not going to end well. Rejection will say, "You will be back; remember last time? Remember when you came running back when you tried to leave this box? The moral of his story is that only you can keep you in the box. My husband tells a powerful story while he is preaching about a monkey who is trying to escape a cage. The story goes something like this; There were some monkey trappers that would put food in a hollow hole. The monkeys were in a dilemma because while they could grab the food, they could not get it out of the trap. The hole is only big enough for the monkey's hand to pass through, but he could not get his hand and the food through that small hole. The monkey panicked because he thought his hand was stuck. He did not realize that all he had to do was let go of the banana and he would free himself.

Isn't that like us with this box? All we have to do is lift the lid and leave but we're holding on to our comfort zones which keep us crippled in the box. All we must do is let go of what we are trying to carry, and we will be free. Let go of people's opinions and we would be free. Let go of people who are not productive for your future. Think about this; the monkey could only be free if he brought his own hand out of the hole. How many people have you tried to bring out of that hole and are stuck there because you will not let them go? The devil does not care who he uses to throw you off track. He will use your parents, your children, best friends, boss, your dog, cat, and your vehicle. He does not care what method he uses to get you to admit defeat. He is a head manipulator and assassin. Satan has a goal every day and that goal is to ruin your life. Whatever he needs to utilize to accomplish that goal, he will do it.

It is easy for people to encourage you when you are going through, but can they celebrate you when you make it out? Be mindful to watch how those in your inner circle move when change hits your house. Some people can only tolerate you if you are struggling. As long as you are a single parent with children by different fathers. As long as you are getting evicted, or your vehicle being repossessed. Or while you are in the welfare line on 12th and Vliet waiting for food stamps and free medical assistance. They can only tolerate you while you are barely making it, but when God elevates you, brings you out, and lifts you up, you need to look around again and see who is still there and if they are clapping. Come out of that box sis or bro. That box will make you claustrophobic. You have been wondering why folks are in your personal business. That is because you are in a box, and they are in your personal space. They are all in your business because you have allowed them to package you and wrap you the way that they saw fit. Come out of the box and be free. Just like the monkey (and no, I am not referring to you as a monkey), he would not let go of what he deemed to be important, that which he deemed to be a prize, and for that reason, he was trapped by his own hand. Be free today and live outside of the box.

Chapter 10:
Smooth Off Burleigh

Words to the wise: Every time I go anywhere to preach, I am sure to let the audience know what they can expect. I am smooth off tenth and Burleigh and there is nothing I can do about it. I grew up in the hood and thus, I am a hood preacher. I said I grew up in the hood but am not ghetto. I have class and God has given me a hood anointing to help His people. What does that mean, preacher? That means that I can relate. I understand poverty. I know the struggles of single parenthood. I have been finessed out of my socks before. I had jokas try to pimp me out of my future. I was almost sex trafficked and manipulated into prostitution. I have been talked about and had my name scandalized. I have been evicted. I had my vehicle repossessed. I have been cheated on. I have been fired from a job or jobs. I know what $4.25 minimum wage is. I know what it is like to walk 20 blocks to work and 20 blocks home. I know what it is like to have several children from different fathers.

I know what it is like to get a $673 welfare check and have to survive. I know what it is like not to be invited. I know what it is like to be shunned by those that are supposed to have your back. I know what it is like to be called a female dog, a whore, slut, a tramp, a homeless female dog, a skank, etc. I know what it is like to be verbally abused, physically abused, sexually abused, you name it. That is why no matter what we encounter in this life, we must lean and depend on the Father because in all that we have gone through and being bent to the point of almost breaking, He held us up to keep us from falling. He held our arms and feet to keep us from snapping in half.

Romans 8:28 shares that all things are working together for our good. No baker can make a cake with just flour. He or she needs several ingredients to make that cake. The struggle is only one ingredient to your cake. Hardship will be another ingredient. Joy is another ingredient. Laughter is another ingredient. Long suffering is another ingredient. New Edition wrote a song that says Sunny days; everybody loves them, tell me baby, can you stand the rain? Storms will come, this we know for sure, tell me baby can you stand the rain? I love this song, especially when Tim Rogers and the Fellas turn it into a gospel track because the rain is what waters our crops. Yes, you have been drenched before, but you did not drown. God wants to know; can you stand the rain? Can you endure the storm? Are you going to complain about your Burleigh season or are you going to rejoice because you made it out of the hood?

I was a peculiar child. I have been talking to God since I was a toddler. I had a vivid imagination, but I knew God heard me. I have gone through times that have been so tough and mentally draining that most people would have given up by now. But God! He is Alpha and the Omega, beginning and the ending, first and the last, King of Kings, Lord of Lords, He is ever present in my time of need, He is all-knowing, all-powerful, He's A consuming fire, He told Moses that he was I am that I am, He's a lawyer in a courtroom, doctor in a sick room, He's a bridge over troubled waters, He's a timeless God, the ancient one, He's a mysterious God, He's a ruler, Zeus was no match for Him, Apollos was no match for Him, Buddha was no match for him, Athena is no match for Him, Brahman is no match for Him, He's Jehovah Gibbor. He makes his enemies sit still. He is a big God!

I have cried countless nights wrestling with my consciousness, but there is one conclusion that I have come to and that is that the Father will give you peace during chaos. When I was going through in my life, walking to the bus stop with three children in a double stroller, cold, hungry, and beaten up by life but trying to have joy in my heart for my children and showing no fear so they would not be scared, it was the Lord that kept my mind at peace. I want to encourage someone who feels that they are at the point of breaking; people are talking about you, you are the topic of discussion at family gatherings, everybody talking about how bad you look, your kids are not kept up, their hair is nappy and they smell like pee, your house isn't the greatest, you live in the hood and have roaches, you don't know who your child's father is, you never graduated high school, you got on those drugs really bad, you may have even had your children taken from you, can I encourage you right there? Can I minister to that valley that you are in, and you are ready to leave? You have taken more losses than you know what to do with and you want to escape. Can I minister to you that greater is your later? You must trust God even when you cannot trace Him. His hand is working even when you cannot feel it. I want to tell you that my hoodness is what keeps me humble. It allows me to have compassion for others. It reminds me of where I came from. I am straight out of the mud, smooth of 10th and Burleigh, 10th and Ring, 10th and Concordia, 15th, and Keefe, 24th Place and Burleigh, and 24th and Townsend. If you are from Milwaukee, Wisconsin and you are reading this book, then you will understand what I am talking about.

The Lord will give you a Burleigh anointing that once He delivers you, you will go back and tell others to come to see a man. If you are reading this and are having a tough time with the ridicule of people, I prophecy that the Lord is going to give you a Bird Man anointing in this season. People are going to find themselves putting some respect on your name. There used to be a time that some of the rumors and labels folks put on me were true, but God has a way of taking what was meant for evil and working that thing out for our good. God put a fire in my spirit to lift the underdogs. Those that have been thrown away like trash and counted out as if you did not matter. His love for us reels us into His bosom. He finds us wherever we are lying dormant, and He heals us. I want to encourage you to never be so far gone that the Father will not receive you back.

I am a firm believer that God changes our ways but can still use our personalities. I'm a certified goofball. I love to laugh and have an enjoyable time. I remember the first time I met my husband, Pastor Cosey, we met at church. Our first date was at El Greco's on Appleton Avenue, we went out to eat and he told me that I could order whatever I wanted, and I did a salad and chicken stir fry. He told me a story about his days having his own security company and I started laughing. I was laughing so hard that I was snorting and crying real tears. I looked over at him and he was crying and laughing too. From that day forward, I knew we were soulmates.

Your personality is unique and distinct. It is one of those things that separates us from the masses. However, Beloved, know that your personality will not gel and vibe with all people. We are commissioned to love one another, but that does not mean that we will always like one another. Some of us attempt to lie about this concept, but that does not mean that it is not true. It is the reason some of us church folks are so fake and phony. You know very well that you do not like some of the ways your sister and brothers in the gospel have, but you refuse to say anything or bring it to your brethren as the Word declares.

Understanding personality differences will allow us to get along better in the kingdom. Rodney King said it best, "Can't we all just get along?" It was a powerful question to use that could also be rhetorical. The crux of the issue is that no matter what our belief systems are, we should be able to get along for the sake of peace, if nothing else. Our Jesus should be the same. If we say that we love Him, we should be able to love each other for the sake of peace.

You do not have to like a person's ways to get along.

<u>Chapter 11:</u>

Walk the Divine Path of the Lord

Word to the wise: May I prophesy to ten thousand of you who will read this book that the next season of struggle in your life will be forced to bless you. We are right in the midst of the COVID pandemic, and it seemed as if death, job loss, and loss of church membership was on a bidden path to cause us to lose everything we have. However, many of us found out that because our God is supreme, even COVID must bless us. The Word of the Lord today is to walk the divine path.

Psalm 37:23 declares that the Lord orders the steps of a good man: and he delights in his way. May I share with you that although you are going through an uncomfortable season in your life, what the devil had planned, will not pan out? Walk the divine path and whatever spoils you encounter on your way; they are free for the taking. There is a buffet of blessings that have been released into the Earth and your hands will not be big enough to carry them all. In fact, may I prophesy to you that you are going to need a sack to store some of the spoils you pick up.

Some of you may be asking, "What are the spoils?" The spoils are the seasons where the harvest was ripe for the picking, but the enemy allowed you to self-sabotage the moment. The new career you were supposed to embark on, but the spirits of fear and rejection caused you not to apply. You should be walking into the freshness of joy and tranquility, but the bitterness of a troubled relationship will not let you be free. Neither will it allow you to progress in peace. The Father is imploring you to walk the divine path, hearken to His voice, and fill your sack.

May I share with you that sometimes when we are walking the divine path, the enemy meets us along the way to intercept our destiny?

The devil comes to steal, kill, and destroy. His mission is to kidnap us on the way to destinies and keep us from obtaining the promise. In this season, while you are walking along the divine path or the spiritual yellow brick road, the devil will try to circumvent your travel. He is like the Wicked Witch of the West that tried to stop Dorothy from going home in the Wizard of Oz. He cannot stand the thought of you being this close to the promise and you have the nerve to be picking up everything he stole along the way.

When the enemy decided to fight you and steal your harvest, he committed an act of war and because you are a soldier in the Lord's army, this meant that Heaven had to respond. Now that you are walking the divine path, the hosts of Heaven are walking with you. Gabriel and Michael are the guard's captains and have come armed with swords, shields, and bucklers. You can pick up the spoils because the Master sent the army to the enemy's camp and put the flip-flips on the devil (them hands). The devil thought he had a capable army until he came up against one more powerful than his own.

God is calling His children back to divine order. This means that He's the tour guide and we look to Him for confirmation and instruction. The Law of thermodynamics indicates that chaos can never produce order. God is a God of order. Even nature cannot create order in a chaotic environment. If you want to reap the blessings along the divine path, you must get in order by submitting to His will, way, and voice. We must submit to God's perfect plan for our lives. We cannot continue to plant cabbages and expect to pick greens when the harvest is ripe. You are what you plant. We cannot continue to plant seeds of disorder, gossip, envy, and jealousy and expect to pick a harvest of peace along the path.

Even nature must line up. That is evident because even grass will grow through concrete simply because it is operating in a productive environment and even a deterrent such as concrete can't stop it from growing. The path is yours to walk, but you need the Lord's guidance concerning what spoils to keep and what spoils to leave. Although some things you lost in your past are available again and attainable, it does not mean you should pick them up. Some spoils are so broken they will serve you no purpose. You will eventually have to throw them away anyway. Walk the path, heed his voice, carry your sack, pick up your spoils, and praise God because He did it again.

Sometimes in life it feels that we are so off course that we are missing the mark and we are missing it often. There have been times in my life when I secluded myself, shut everybody out, and consciously decided to refocus because I needed more of the Lord. The mercies of the Lord are Yea and Amen. This is why walking the divine path of the Lord is essential in the life of a Christian. Where would we go without his guidance? How would we stand without Him holding us up? Where would we go without his direction? The bible declares that the Lord orders the steps of a good man, and it will be essential through the storms of life for the Lord to lead us and guide us.

Storms are uncomfortable. I remember driving down I85 leaving Charlotte. The weather conditions started with powerful winds that rocked the car back and forth. While driving, my husband and I could see debris on the road. Branches of trees that had blown into the roadway, trash that blew from its resting place on the side of the road, worn tires that were left in the road from tractor-trailers that experienced blowouts flew underneath the vehicle. The rain was beating on the vehicle so fierce that it left the windshield wipers defective and rendered useless. Then the damage happened. Just as the storm was blowing around us, we ran over something in the road that made the loudest sound I have ever heard in my life. It scared us both. We had no idea what we ran over, but we knew we hit something huge.

When we arrived home, we went straight to bed. The storm delayed our destination. A journey that should have taken us four hours, due to the elements, caused us to get home in six. When we got up the next morning, we inspected our vehicle because we knew that something impacted our vehicle's undercarriage during the storm. The driver's side had damage right underneath the door. The underbelly was cracked in the middle. The vehicle's rear in the bumper area was pulled outwards instead of inwards. This led me to believe that we ran over something huge that was lying in the road. My sticky suspicion says that we ran over a deer that lay in the roadway after it was hit by another vehicle.

You may be asking yourself, why is the author putting such a great emphasis on the storm and the damage that came out of it? I am glad you asked that question. Storms can only brew during certain conditions. I shared with you that the wind started blowing, but I omitted to let you know that we could smell the rain in the air. In addition, thunder was in the clouds. We knew that a powerful storm was coming, and it was unavoidable. We were driving right into it. In addition, there was nothing we could do to stop the wind from rocking our truck from back and forth because we were in the thick of the storm. We were right in the center of it, and we could not turn around and go back the other way. We had to trust the GPS and go right through it.

In the south, whenever there is torrential rain and the weather conditions suggest that a powerful storm is making its way through the area, the semi-trucks will cruise the farthest lane to the right and turn their hazards on to signal other drivers to exercise caution. When there is a torrential downpour, all the other passenger vehicles also turn their hazards on. The hazard lights alert the vehicle behind you that although they cannot see the make, model, or color of the vehicle ahead of them, they can see the warning lights flashing on the back of the vehicle in front of them. It alerts other drivers that there is a vehicle in front of you, slow your speed, and exercise caution in a storm. Jesus is the hazard signal during a storm. Although we cannot see our way when we are going through the storm, He is leading the way so that we can follow Him out of it.

I know that there have been some storms in your life that have caused damage to your personal being. I know you have wrestled with depression because you have lost things while amid the storm. I know that you have given up hope because the rain has been beating down on you, so that your internal defenses that would help you navigate the rain have been rendered useless. I know that your last relationship broke you and caused you to suffer emotionally, physically, and mentally, but did you pay attention to the warning lights ahead? Did you know that right in the midst of the storm, the Father was signaling to you son, daughter, over here! I want you to know that God has a way of escape for you. He desires to help you navigate the tough times in our lives. He wants to help us. Do you desire the Father's help or do you want to fight the rain alone?

<u>Chapter 12:</u>

Lessons from our Pain

Word to the wise: I have never understood why such a loving Father would allow His children to experience pain. What is the lesson in suffering? What is it that we are supposed to gain from pain? Why is it so hard to overcome pain and find pleasure, joy, hope, or vindication? I have come to realize that this journey is not easy, and we are on the Earth to become well-rounded individuals and learn fruitful lessons concerning life. The bible declares that the angels do not have this testimony. They have never known about heartache or depression. They have never known the fear of leaving an unhealthy relationship and being all alone. They have never experienced losing a loved one and having to make funeral arrangements. Or, having to clean out their houses and manage an estate. The angels do not have the testimony of a soul on the Earth.

Pain teaches us lessons that without it, we would have never learned. Pain hurts. It tears at the unique fabric of the individual and causes them to experience sorrow. Pain is not a feeling that anyone desires to embrace. No one that is a well-rounded or balanced individual desires to feel pain. One would have to be crazy, fresh off the looney farm to sign up for a lesson in pain. When we go through pain, we should never give directly into the emotion without understanding the true lesson we should take away from it.

I can remember residing with my mom on 24th and Townsend. We lived in a beautiful abode. It was a four-bedroom house complete with a living room, dining room, and a den in the front of the home. There was a complete basement, although it was not finished but it was clean. My sister had her own room, I shared a room with my little sister Jamiee, and my brothers James and Jeremy had their own room. I had two children at the time, Gabriel, and Heaven, and was pregnant with my son Amyyr.

It was tax season and I remember going up to 76th and Hampton and purchasing an 89 Buick Toronado. It was a two-door, V6, fully loaded, all leather, burgundy in color vehicle. I remember being so proud that I bought this vehicle. I was promoted to shift manager at McDonalds and had just received a ten-cent raise. I thought to myself, man, God is really blessing me. He is looking out for me in ways that I cannot imagine. I had just given my mother some money because I was an adult, and it was her house.

I was out shopping for my kids and had just returned home. I went into the house, put some bags down and decided that I was going to take a nap. That is when my sister ran into the room and said there was a fire in the attic. We called the fire department and tried our best to put it out, but it was already burning the insulation and spreading quickly. Nothing in the attic on the second floor could have sparked a flame, and we believe the fire was electrical. We started running out of the house. We called my mom who was at work at McDonalds on 27th and Capital and told her that the house was on fire. By the time my mom got there, it was fully engulfed in the back of the house.

The fire department was working to get the fire put out quickly. We started praying and asking the Lord not to allow us to lose everything. We had lost everything: pictures, report cars, baby announcements, childhood memories, dolls, keepsakes. Everything in the basement was gone. Every item of clothing was waiting to be washed. Baby seats, baby toys, high school diplomas, high school cap and gowns with tassels, prom dresses, everything was gone.

The next day we returned to the house to salvage anything that we could. It was so sad watching my mom go into her house and try to save things that she worked so hard to obtain. We were not rich or well-off people, so we cherished the wonderful things the good Lord did permit us to buy. Family members were showing up and trying to help us salvage all that we could. I remember my cousins saying, "Don't cry Aunt Jan; it's going to be alright." I believe that my mother, a devout woman of faith, knew that already and she had faith in God that He would restore all that she lost, but nevertheless, the pain of seeing all that you own go up in flames and having to start all over again was not a good feeling.

I have often asked the Master, what was the lesson in all of this? Why did we have to lose everything to gain again? Why would you allow our home to burn up as poor as we were? Why does everything bad happen to people who are good and especially those who serve you and praise your holy name? We go to church every Sunday, sing songs of Zion, we dance before your throne, we kneel at your altar, and we bend our knees and pray and hearts to do your will. Why would you allow such a travesty to intercept our path?

The Master answered me in my consciousness and said, "Daughter, what I have done before, I have the power to do again. Only this time will I do it the greater for my own glory. No man can do what I have done; for that matter, great will be thy testimony. What the Father promised happened. My mom moved into another place on 95th and Brown Deer Road. A tri-level condominium, but that was not the greatest victory. Everyone involved in the fire went on to do abundant things.

My mom moved to South Carolina and bought her first house. She has the best house on the block. She bought a brand-new car. She was even relocated from Milwaukee, Wisconsin, to Florence, South Carolina, by the company she worked for. Isn't that a blessing that only the Father could do? I now reside in Atlanta, Georgia. My husband and I bought our first home and a brand-new car with 5 miles on it right off the lot. The devil is a whole lie. I graduated with my bachelor's degree and was accepted into University of Georgia School of Law shortly after. What God has ordained for us is for us. No fire can keep Him from reigning. No loss can keep a child of the living God from praising.

So, what was the lesson in all of this? 1 Peter 5:7 admonishes us to cast all our cares on the Lord, for he cares for you. It goes further in verse 8 to be sober, be vigilant; because your adversary, the devil, as a roaring lion, walketh about, seeking whom he may devour. The lesson is, can you trust God during travesty? Can you trust Him when you lose everything? Do you trust Him to give you double for your trouble or will you murmur and complain about the season that you are in? God wanted to see if we would trust Him in all things.

If you are reading this book, I would like to pose this question. What is the worst season that you have ever experienced in your life? What moment has caused you to have the most severe depression you have ever experienced in your life? What caused that depression? What is the root of that depression? Did you ever get an apology after the event? Did you ever recover after the event? What was your first course of action after it occurred? Did you call on the Master for guidance or did you become angry because it happened to you?

Our first posture should always be prayer and supplication. We often jump to conclusions and react out of our emotions rather than giving God thanks. 1 Thessalonians 5:18 implores us to give thanks in everything. Everything simply means in all things. There should not be a moment in our existence where we fail to give God thanks. I am not a novice. I understand that sometimes it is hard to give thanks, especially when you do not know why you are being attacked and what you are experiencing makes it hard to be thankful. It is hard to give thanks when you do understand why you have experienced such a great loss. It is hard to give thanks when you go out of your way to be good to folks and they still stab you in your back. God has a plan for our sorrows. We may not understand at the moment why things happen the way that they do, but the Father is all-knowing and all-powerful. Nothing catches him off guard and He certainly is not thrown off by our woes, but He wants to have confidence in us that we will trust Him when life disappoints us.

We must have this confidence in Him that even though tragedy may befall us, we know that all our help comes from Him. We must learn to trust God's plan even when we do not understand it. Romans 8: 28 shares with us that, "All things are working together for our good." The good, the bad, and the ugly. It is all working out with precision timing for our good. It is just like making a cake; eggs alone are bitter, and they do not have an acquired taste by themselves. Flour is a starch; it is chalky by itself. However, when we mix flour, and eggs, with other ingredients topped with frosting makes a fabulous dessert. I want to encourage you today that despite whatever valley you have experienced in your life or the low place that you may be experiencing even now, to trust God. Do not give up on Him because He cares for you. Just as surely as you entered that uncomfortable place, He's already made a way of escape for you. He's already provided a door for you to travel through. Trust God.

Chapter 13:

Return to Sender

Word to the wise, sometimes we face challenges in our lives that leave us on the fence concerning certain areas of our development. Can I minister to five thousand of you that will read this book that the Father has more in store for you than the disrespect that you have been allowing? What is it about you that causes a person to go to great lengths to tear down your sense of self-worth, to try to void all your accomplishments, and utterly attempt to ruin your character and your witness?

Beloved, you have entered a crux in your life, where you have come to the intersection of a disrespectful boulevard and front street. Why have we consistently allowed people to disrespect us and front on us straight? Do you know what front means, right? Frontin, Mc Breed wrote a song that said, "Ain't no future in your fronting." Frontin, to stunt on you, to publicly embarrass you, to put up a facade or make appearances. The urban dictionary defines fronting as typically trying to impress or in some way deceive or maintain an image. This is what people do when they front. They will embarrass you to impress others. Aren't you tired of being fronted on? How long will you tolerate the disrespect?

You are entering a season of your life where you must disallow disrespect!

81

You must get to a place where you refuse to declare it valid, to veto it, and to refuse to admit truth or validity concerning disrespect. You must completely refuse to allow the veracity of the system of disrespect. The devil does not play fair when it comes to disrespect. He will allow you to be disrespected and remove your voice so you cannot defend yourself. Disrespect knows no boundaries. It does not care who it offends, who it attacks, and who becomes hurt by it. Disrespect is as disrespect does. This is why you cannot allow yourself to be disrespected.

You must return everything sent your way not like the Father to the sender. Disallow that seed from entering your mailbox. In order for mail that does not belong to you to enter your abode, you must first pick it up out of the mailbox and bring it into your home. If you are like me, you have USPS Daily Digest that appears in your email every day that notifies you of mail that is scheduled to be delivered to your residence that day. This is prophetic. In this season, the Spirit of Truth is going to forewarn us regarding every attack that is on its way to us. He is going to notify you by way of spiritual notification that hate is on the way, envy is on the way, slander is on the way, jealousy is on the way, sabotage is on the way, and a package from Snakes'R'Us is on the way to you. Before that attack even hits your mailbox, you ought to run before the mail carrier pulls off and say, "Excuse me, Sir or Ma'am, this person no longer lives here." You must get to a place where you return it to the sender and not feel bad about it.

You must curb disrespect, send it to your junk mail folder and then dump the entire folder in the trash. Why are you holding onto someone else's mail? Every day I receive mail in my box addressed to Paula Coleman. Apparently, prior to us moving in, she was a former resident. I get all sorts of junk mail, advertisements, bills, and unwanted items in the name of Paula Coleman. I have started leaving them in the mailbox and allowing the mail lady to take them back with her. Eventually, the postal service will get the message that

Paula Coleman no longer resides at this address and block any mail addressed to her from making it to the truck.

You must get to where you uninvite disrespect. Sometimes we get disrespected because people think it is cute and feel like they can. The longer you allow people to walk all over you like your name is Welcome and you are a mat, they will. The moment that you demand respect, and they know that if they want a relationship with you, it will not be tolerated, they will stop. I dare you to uninvite the disrespect. Stop inviting it in. Stop answering the phone call for people who you know are calling to check on you, talk down to you, emotionally and mentally abuse you and put some respect on your own name. Some conversations that you have will be uncomfortable at first because you have become accustomed to not having a voice, but the moment you learn to start putting your foot down and command respect is the moment you'll begin to get it.

Do not allow yourself to be disrespected so long that you take your frustrations out on everyone who needs to have a meaningful and challenging conversation with you. Just because a brother, sister or spouse needs to challenge you in an area does not mean it is disrespectful. It is called mutual understanding. You may agree to disagree, but it is still a mutual understanding and conversation that leads to open-mindedness and respect at the end of it. However, if you see disrespect as someone having a difference of opinion, you are dead wrong. If you are the only one whose opinion matters, you can be classified as a narcissist. A difference of opinion is just what it is. However, an individual is going to be a free thinker who can think for themselves. That means that even if they love you, they do have a say and even if you disagree with what their say is, you still have to respect it.

Nullify the disrespect. We are entering a season where we are undoing the factions of disrespect that have been allowed to take root in us. God is not about to play concerning you. You have value, you have a purpose, and you deserve to be respected.

Chapter14:

He will turn your pain into purpose

Word to the wise: I remember being a young girl and struggling with familial issues like not liking my stepfather, going to live with my Aunt Merl or my sister Yolonda and her husband, and being out of control. Sometimes I would leave home and go to my Aunt Merl's house to escape my home life. How many of us know that sometimes as bad as we try to make our home life seem, we have a hand in some of it? Sometimes God allows us to experience some hard places in order to mature and develop us.

There was this old graveyard at the intersection 20th and Hopkins. We lived off 24th and Townsend; my Aunt Merl lives off 10th and Ring. I would often walk to Aunt Merl's house and use that graveyard as a cut-through. I used to look at the headstones and read the names, the date of birth and the date of death, and ponder what kind of person the deceased was. Were they kind to people? Did they have children? Did they die a premature death? Did they know that their time was up on the earth? Lastly, did they make peace with people who were their enemies, and did they have a relationship with the Father?

I have always been a very peculiar person and have always tried to analyze life to find its true meaning. Walking through that graveyard was peaceful because there are a couple of things the dead will not do and cannot do, judge and talk about you. The dead have nothing to say when you are passing by their tombstone. In fact, the last remnants of who they once were are laying 6 feet beneath the dirt. They have no opinion about your life. They do not know your past history and what pain you have encountered. To be honest, the dead do not even care. They are lifeless and all but a memory. However, at a time when I felt like I did not have anyone, I had dead friends. I could talk and they would not talk back.

There came a time in my life where it seemed as if I had enemies galore and I could not figure out if it was sheer jealousy or if people were trying to find a reason not to like me. I remember walking to the 27-bus stop to go to high school. I thought I had friends across the street by the names of Muffy and Moo Moo. They were sisters. Their mother had a drug addiction, and it was so sad to see their mom that way. I remember playing with them from sun up to sundown. Then one summer, I got hired at Bachman's furniture on 68th and Capitol Drive. I started coming up, if you will. I bought my first pair of white K-Swiss classics with black stripes. I had money, so I thought. I started buying those things I liked. My second purchase was a percolator house mixtape from DJ Screw. I was always an exceptionally good dancer and had been dancing since the age of at least 6 or 7. Well, one day after we had finished dancing in front of the house, Muffy and Moo Moo must not have had enough of the percolator because they stole my tape. Did I ask which one stole it. They lied to my face knowing that we were the only ones in the front dancing, and they had just asked me to borrow it and I said no. I advised them that I no longer desired to be their friends because I did not want friends that were thieves or liars. Well, you can say from that day forward, I was public enemy number one. That feud lasted for 3 years, and I fought their cousin Crystal after she kept antagonizing me and threatening me. From that point on, they constantly tried to jump me on the way to school. My mother used to wait on the porch with a baseball bat wishing a joker would.

One day, I was walking home from the bus stop when my sister Yolonda picked me up. We ran into their cousin on the way home and my sister asked her if she still wanted to fight. The girl was like yes and ran home to get her people. My sister and I pulled up at the house and everybody was ready to throw hands. We called ourselves putting an end to the feud. I have never seen so many people come out of a house. Almost like roaches. Everybody was fighting and because there were more of them than us, we ended up getting jumped lol. My Uncle Greg got knocked out by some young dudes and my sister Trina got jumped by one of the cousins and the crackhead Moma. However, Trina was holding her weight and throwing sheer licks popping everybody. I guess you really cannot say she got jumped because after the Moma got her eye dotted, she disappeared from the mele never to be seen again.

I was popping whoever I could. These heffas tormented me for three years. I'm getting my licks in. It got so bad my cousins came over from Burleigh, who had straps. They were about to light 24th Townsend up. Later in the evening, there was a drive-by, and somebody got shot on that side of the street. I guess they had more enemies than just us. Somebody is reading this and saying I thought she was a preacher. You must realize that I was 16 or 17 at the time of this occurrence. I had not accepted my call yet, so just laugh with me while I go back down memory lane. I guess all that fighting did not solve a thing because I never got my percolator tape back. (Laughing but profoundly serious). Sometimes when I look back on my life as I approach the 42nd year of my time on this earth, I get the giggles thinking about the times I should have just shut up and said less. I also thank God that he preserved my life and kept me so that I have the ability to giggle. The devil is a whole lie out here in these streets.

<u>Chapter 15:</u>

But Did you Die? Naw, You overcame it!

Words to the wise: Sometimes life forces you to re-evaluate some choices you have made and some areas you have been. I am smooth off Burleigh, so the first question I ask myself is, "But did you die?" Have you ever gone through so much that you thought you were going to die because it hurt so bad, but you have to snap out of it and ask yourself, "But did you die?" I want to encourage you that I do not care how bad it hurts; you are alive to feel the pain. You still have an opportunity to overcome it, to rebound from it, and outlive it.

Sometimes when you see the attack coming, you literally have to outrun it. You must have a roadrunner anointing. When you see the snake's fangs, you ought to fly past it and say meet. You have to come to an agreement with yourself to let the devil know not today. Allow me to minister to you that sometimes, the Holy Ghost will warn you that an attack is coming and unfortunately, this is one that you are going to have to learn from. There is no reason to continue repeating exams to which you already have the answers. How does one fail an open-book test? Could it be that they were too lazy to look for the right answer or they just clearly did not care?

Sis, Bro, you did not die. It could not kill you. It bent you but it did not break you. It wounded you but you are still winning. It hurt you but it did not hinder you. It inflicted pain on you but it could not keep you from purpose. The next time that you decide that you are going to complain about the pain, ask yourself, "But did you die?" Did it kill you? Did it hinder you?? Were you upset? Of course, you were, but being upset does not equal defeat. The reality of the matter is you did not die! You overcame it and you are victorious. What can that ole sleuth footed; knock-kneed, cock-eyed devil do to you? If God is for you, He is more than the world against you. Nothing by any means shall harm you.

Revelation 12: 11: And they overcame him by the blood of the Lamb, and by the word of their testimony; and they loved not their lives unto the death.

About the Author

Pastor Prophet Nekisha L. Cosey is a prolific speaker, dynamic orator, and powerhouse Prophet. She is known for her down to earth kingdom approach, creative analogies, and deliverance ministry gifting. A native of Milwaukee, Wisconsin, she is married to Pastor Nicholas E. Cosey Sr. She is the mother of 8 children, four boys, four girls, and 2 grandchildren. She accepted her call to preach at the age of 19 and has been preaching for over 23 years. She holds a Bachelor of Science in Management and is presently attending the University of Georgia School of Law completing her Masters in the Study of Law, Class of 2023. Pastor Nekisha was born to repair the breach in our paths to destiny. She is an end time gift called to set the captives free. She has a heart and love for the Father's children and her desire is to see their shines restored. Pastor Nekisha believes that we as God's representatives in the Earth, hold no power of our own, but the power the Father has equipped us with. We are all a "Living Representation of the Dumanis Power!" She was born to remind the enemy that Hell shall be his resting place and Heaven our home."

Instagram: PastorProphetCosey

Facebook: Nekisha Cosey Ministries

Email: NekishaCoseyMinistries@gmail.com

CPSIA information can be obtained
at www.ICGtesting.com
Printed in the USA
BVHW050457100323
660081BV00012B/1015